Crochet
PATTERNS & PROJECTS

Publications International, Ltd.

Consultant: Heidi Beazley

Written by Beth Taylor

Photo styling by Amy Stark

Photography by Christopher Hiltz

Additional photography © Shutterstock.com, Thinkstock

Crochet symbols and abbreviations source:
Craft Yarn Council's www.YarnStandards.com

Louis Weber, CEO
Publications International, Ltd.
7373 North Cicero Avenue
Lincolnwood, Illinois 60712

www.pilbooks.com

Permission is never granted for commercial purposes.

ISBN: 978-1-4508-8257-6

Manufactured in China.

8 7 6 5 4 3 2 1

Table of Contents

Pattern Basics
ABBREVIATIONS, SYMBOLS & GAUGE

Abbreviations & Symbols

Crochet patterns often use abbreviations and symbols as shorthand to represent frequently used stitches and techniques. Use the guide below as you start to follow patterns using shorthand.

Abbreviations

alt	alternate
approx	appoximately
beg	begin/beginning
bet	between
BL	back loop(s)
bo	bobble
BP	back post
BPdc	back post double crochet
BPsc	back post single crochet
BPtr	back post treble crochet
CC	contrasting color
ch	chain(s)
ch-sp	chain space
CL	cluster
cm	centimeter(s)
cont	continue
dc	double crochet
dec	decrease(s)/decreasing
dtr	double treble
edc	extended double crochet
ehdc	extended half double crochet
esc	extended single crochet
FL	front loop(s)
FP	front post
FPdc	front post double crochet
FPtr	front post treble crochet
hdc	half double crochet
hk	hook
inc	increase(s)/increasing
lp(s)	loop(s)
MC	main color
mm	millimeter(s)

p	picot
pc	popcorn
pat(s)	pattern(s)
pm	place marker
prev	previous
rem	remain/remaining
rep	repeat(s)
rnd(s)	round(s)
RS	right side
sc	single crochet
sl st	slip stitch
sk	skip
sp(s)	space(s)
st(s)	stitch(es)
tch	turning chain
tog	together
tr	treble crochet
WS	wrong side
yd(s)	yard(s)
yo	yarn over
"	inch(es)
[ ]	work instructions within brackets as many times as directed
( )	work instructions within parentheses as many times as directed
*	repeat the instructions following the single asterisk as directed
**	repeat the instructions between asterisks as many times as directed or repeat from a given set of instructions

Symbols

⬯	chain
•	slip stitch
X or †	single crochet
	half double crochet
	double crochet
	treble crochet
	sc2tog
	sc3tog
	dc2tog
	dc3tog
	3-dc cluster
	3-hdc cluster/ puff st/bobble
	5-dc popcorn
	5-dc shell
	ch-3 picot
	front post dc
	back post dc
	worked in back loop only**
	worked in front loop only**

**Symbol appears at base of stitch being worked.

Gauge

Gauge refers to how many stitches and rows you should have in a given area in order to match the measurements of a project. The pattern will state how many stitches and rows are needed to achieve the proper gauge. For the projects in this book, gauge is not important. It's most important when making clothing items, like sweaters or socks, in order to get the proper fit.

Four things determine your gauge:

- Tension (how loosely or tightly you form the stitches)
- Type and weight of the yarn
- Size of the hook
- Stitch being worked

Making your gauge swatch

Using the same yarn, hook size, and stitch you plan to use for the pattern, crochet a swatch at least 4 x 4 in. If the project has specific gauge instructions, follow those. After your gauge swatch is complete, lay it on a flat surface.

Measuring your gauge swatch

Use a ruler, measuring tape, or gauge tool and measure 4 inches across your swatch and mark it with pins. Count the number of stitches between the pins. This is your stitch gauge.

Next you will need to measure the row gauge. Place your measuring tool vertically on the swatch, measure 4 inches, and mark it with pins. Count the number of rows between the pins. This is your row gauge.

Adjusting your gauge

If your gauge swatch has too many stitches or rows compared to the pattern, use a larger hook. If your gauge swatch doesn't have enough stitches or rows, use a smaller hook. Keep adjusting your hook size until you have the required gauge.

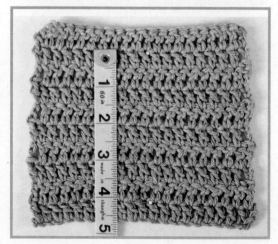

Tip: The stitch gauge is more important than the row gauge. That's because it is easier to adjust the number of rows than to adjust the number of stitches in your crochet project.

Patterns

GRANNY SQUARES, MOTIFS & STITCHES

Traditional Granny Square

Stitches Used
Chain stitch (ch), **double crochet** (dc), **slip stitch** (sl st)

Instructions

Ch 6, join the ends of the ch with sl st to form a ring.

Round 1: Ch 3 (counts as first dc), then work 2 dc in center of the ring, ch 3. Now work [3 dc in center of the ring, ch 3] 2 times. Sl st in top of beg ch 3 to join. Fasten off.

Round 2: Join 2nd color with sl st in one of the ch-3 corner sps. Ch 3 (counts as first dc), then work (2 dc, ch 3, 3 dc) in the same corner sp as join, ch 1. Now work [3 dc, ch 3, 3 dc, in next ch-3 corner sp, ch 1] 2 times. Sl st in top of beg ch 3 to join. Fasten off.

Round 3: Join 3rd color with sl st in one of the ch-3 corner sps. Ch 3 (counts as first dc), then work (2 dc, ch 3, 3 dc) in the same corner sp as join, ch 1. Now work [3 dc in the ch-1 sp from the prev rnd, ch 1, 3 dc, ch 3, 3 dc in the next ch-3 corner sp, ch 1] 2 times. Work 3 dc in the last ch-1 sp from prev rnd, ch 1. Sl st in top of beg ch 3 to join. Fasten off.

Round 4: Join 4th color with sl st in one of the ch-3 corner sps. Ch 3 (counts as first dc), then work (2 dc, ch 3, 3 dc) in the same corner sp as join, ch 1. Now work [3 dc, ch 1 in each ch-1 sp from the prev rnd. 3 dc, ch 3, 3 dc in the next ch-3 corner sp, ch 1] 2 times. Work (3 dc, ch 1) in each ch-1 sp from prev rnd, ch 1. Sl st in top of beg ch 3 to join. Fasten off. Weave in yarn tails.

Tip: Use scraps of leftover yarn to make a variety of granny squares in different colors for a fun and colorful afghan.

Modified Granny Square

Stitches Used

Chain stitch (ch), **double crochet** (dc), **single crochet** (sc), **slip stitch** (sl st)

Instructions

Ch 6, join with sl st in first ch to form a ring.

Round 1: Ch 5, [3 dc, ch 2] 3 times in ring, join with sl st in 3rd ch of beg ch 5.

Round 2: Ch 1, sc in same st, [4 sc in ch-2 sp, sc in each of the next 3 dc] 3 times, 4 sc in next ch-2 sp, sc in each of next 2 dc, join with sl st in first sc.

Round 3: Ch 1, sc in same st and next st, [ch 5, sk 2 sts, sc in each of next 5 sts] 3 times, ch 5, sk 2 sts, sc in next 3 sts, join with sl st in first sc.

Round 4: Sl st in next 2 sts and in first ch-5 sp, ch 3 (counts as first dc now and in future rnds), 2 dc in same sp, ch 2, 3 dc in same sp, *ch 2, sk 2 sc, dc in next sc, ch 2, sk 2 sc, (3 dc, ch 2, 3 dc) in next ch-5 sp; rep from * 2 more times, ch 2, sk 2 sc, dc in next sc, ch 2, sk 2 sc, join with sl st in top of beg ch 3.

Round 5: Ch 3, dc in each of next 2 sts, *(3 dc, ch 2, 3 dc) in ch-2 sp, dc in each of next 3 sts, 2 dc in ch-2 sp, ch 1, sk 1 dc, 2 dc in next ch-2 sp ** dc in each of next 3 sts; rep from * around with last rep ending at **, join with sl st in top of beg ch 3.

Round 6: Sl st over to first ch-2 sp, ch 3, (2 dc, ch 2, 3 dc) in same sp, [*sk 1 st, dc in next st, dc in skipped st *; rep from * across to ch-1 sp, dc in ch-1 sp, rep from * across to corner ch-2 sp, (3 dc, ch 2, 3 dc) in corner ch-2 sp]; rep [ ] 3 times, join with sl st in top of beg ch 3. Fasten off.

Tip: You can join multiple granny squares together to make afghans, scarves, pillows, bags, and other accessories.

Spiked Square

Instructions

Change colors every 2 rows.

Ch 22 (or a multiple of 10 sts + 2).

Base row: 1 sc in 2nd ch from hook, 1 sc in next and each ch to end of row. Ch 1, turn.

Row 1: 1 sc in first and each st to end of row. Ch 1, turn.

Row 2: 1 sc in first st, *1 Ssc over each of next 5 sts, 1 sc in each of next 5 sts; rep from * to end of row, finishing with 1 sc in last sc. Ch 1, turn.

Row 3: Rep row 1.

Row 4: Rep row 2.

Row 5: Rep row 1.

Row 6: Rep row 2.

Row 7: Rep row 1.

Row 8: Rep row 2.

Row 9: Rep row 1.

Row 10: 1 sc in first st. *1 sc in each of the next 5 sts, 1 Ssc over each of the next 5 sts; rep from * to end of row, finishing with 1 sc in last sc.

Row 11: Rep row 9.

Row 12: Rep row 10.

Row 13: Rep row 9.

Row 14: Rep row 10.

Row 15: Rep row 9.

Row 16: Rep row 10.

Rep rows 1–16 until desired size.

Edging (optional):
Add double crochet edging around square.

Tip: How to make the Ssc
Insert hook below next st 1 row down (i.e., in the same place as that st was worked), yo, draw lp through and up to height of present row, yo, draw through both lps on hook.

Smooth Wave

Stitches Used

Chain stitch (ch), **double crochet** (dc), **single crochet** (sc), **slip stitch** (sl st)

Instructions

Using color A, ch 28 (or a multiple of 8 sts + 4).

Row 1: Using color A, sk 2 ch (counts as 1 sc), 1 sc in each of the next 3 ch, *1 dc in each of the next 4 ch, 1 sc in each of the next 4 ch; rep from * to end of row. Ch 1, turn.

Row 2: Using color A, sk first st, 1 sc in each of the next 3 sts, *1 dc in each of the next 4 sts, 1 sc in each of the next 4 sts; rep from * to end, working last st in the top of tch. Ch 3, turn.

Row 3: Using color B, sk first st, 1 dc in each of the next 3 sts, *1 sc in each of the next 4 sts, 1 dc in each of the next 4 sts; rep from * to end, working last st in top of tch. Ch 3, turn.

Row 4: Rep row 3.

Rows 5–6: Rep row 2.

Rows 7–8: Rep row 3.

Rows 9–10: Rep row 2.

Rows 11–12: Rep row 3.

Rows 13–14: Rep row 2.

Rows 15–16: Rep row 3.

Rows 17–18: Rep row 2.

Edging (optional):
Stitch a row of sc around edges, working 3 sc in each corner to turn.

Tip: This stitch makes a great baby blanket! Try adding additional colors to the pattern too.

Fisherman's Ring

Stitches Used

Chain stitch (ch), **double crochet** (dc), **single crochet** (sc), **slip stitch** (sl st), **treble crochet** (tr)

Instructions

Make a magic circle.

Round 1: Ch 3, (working inside magic circle) work 15 dc in the circle, pull tail of magic circle to tighten and join with sl st in top of beg ch 3.

Round 2: Ch 1, sc in same st as joining, ch 5, sk 2 dc, sc in next dc, turn, sc in each of the 5 ch, turn, sc in the 2nd skipped dc, *ch 5, sk next unworked dc, sc in the next dc, turn, sc in each of the 5 ch, turn, sc (behind cable), in last skipped dc; rep from * 5 times; ch 5, sc (in front of first cable) in the first skipped dc of the rnd, turn, sc in each of the 5 ch, turn, join with sl st in the first sc (8 cables).

Round 3: Ch 1, sc in same st as joining; *ch 5, sk next 5 sc in cable, sc in the next sc at base of next cable; rep from * around, finishing with ch 5, join with sl st in first sc.

Round 4: Sl st in the first ch-5 sp, ch 3 to count as the first dc, work 4 more dc in same ch-5 sp; *5 dc in the next ch-5 sp; rep from * around; join with sl st in the top of beg ch 3.

Round 5: Ch 1, sc in the same st as joining, ch 5, sk 2 dc, sc in the next dc, turn, sc in each of the 5 ch, turn, sc in the 2nd skipped dc, *ch 5, sk next unworked dc, sc in next dc, turn, sc in each of the 5 ch, turn, sc (behind cable) in last skipped dc; rep from * 17 times, ch 5, sc (in front of first cable) in first skipped dc of the rnd, turn, sc in each of the 5 ch, turn, join with sl st in first sc (20 cables).

Round 6: Ch 1, sc in same st as joining; [ch 5, sk next 5 sc in cable, sc in next sc at base of next cable] 19 times; ch 2, join with dc in the first sc.

Rounds 7–8: Continued on next page.

Round 7: Ch 4 to count as first tr, work 3 more tr in same sp (around post of the last dc in rnd 6), *3 dc in next ch-5 sp, [3 sc in next ch-5 sp] 2 times, 3 dc in next ch-5 sp, 7 tr in next ch-5 sp; rep from * 2 times; 3 dc in next ch-5 sp, [3 sc in next ch-5 sp] 2 times, 3 dc in next ch-5 sp, 3 tr in first ch-5 sp; join with sl st in top of beg ch 4.

Round 8: Ch 1, 2 sc in same st as joining, [sc in each of the next 18 sts, 3 sc in the next tr] 3 times, sc in each of next 18 sts, sc in same st as first sc; join with sl st in first sc. Fasten off.

Mesh Stitch

Stitches Used

Chain stitch (ch), **double crochet** (dc), **half double crochet** (hdc)

Instructions

Ch 29 (or a multiple of 3 sts + 8).

Row 1: Sk 7 ch, *1 dc in next ch, ch 2, sk 2 ch; rep from * to last st, 1 dc in last ch. Ch 5, turn.

Row 2: Sk first dc, *1 dc in next dc, ch 2, sk 2 ch; rep from * to last st, 1 dc in 3rd ch of tch. Ch 5, turn.

Rep row 2 until desired size.

Edging (optional):
Add hdc border.

Tip: Because of all the spaces in this stitch, it works up quickly!

Petal Stitch

Stitches Used
Chain stitch (ch), **single crochet** (sc), **treble crochet** (tr)

Instructions

Ch 17 (or a multiple of 8 sts + 1).

Row 1: 1 sc in 2nd ch from hook, *ch 2, sk 3 ch, 4 tr in next ch, ch 2, sk 3 ch, 1 sc in next ch; rep from * to end of row. Ch 1, turn.

Row 2: 1 sc in first st, *ch 3, sk 2 ch and 1 tr, 1 sc in next tr, ch 3, sk 2 tr and 2 ch, 1 sc in next sc; rep from * to end of row. Ch 4, turn.

Row 3: 1 tr in first st, *ch 2, sk 3 ch, 1 sc in next sc, ch 2, sk 3 ch, 4 tr in next sc; rep from * to end, omitting 1 tr at end of last rep. Ch 1, turn.

Row 4: 1 sc in first st, *ch 3, sk 2 tr and 2 ch, 1 sc in next sc, ch 3, sk 2 ch and 1 tr, 1 sc in next tr; rep from * to end of row. Ch 1, turn.

Row 5: 1 sc in first st, *ch 2, sk 3 ch, 4 tr in next sc, ch 2, sk 3 ch, 1 sc in next sc; rep from * to end of row.

Rep rows 2–5 until desired size.

Edging (optional):
Stitch a single crochet edging around your square, working 3 single crochet stitches in the corners.

African Flower

Stitches Used

Chain stitch (ch), **double crochet** (dc), **single crochet** (sc), **slip stitch** (sl st)

Instructions

Make a magic circle.

Round 1: Ch 3, (working inside magic circle) 1 dc, ch 1, *2 dc, ch 1; rep from * until there are 6 of the dc pairs and 6 ch-sps. Pull beg tail of magic circle to tighten, sl st in top ch of beg ch 3 and fasten off.

Round 2: Change color. Start in a ch-1 sp, ch 5, 2 dc in same sp, *(ch 1, 2 dc, ch 2, 2 dc) in next sp; rep from * 5 times, 1 dc and sl st in 3rd ch of the beg rnd.

Round 3: Ch 3, 6 dc in the ch-2 sp, ch 1, *7 dc in next ch-2 sp, ch 1; rep from * 5 times. Sl st in top ch of beg ch 3. Fasten off.

Round 4: Change color. Ch 1, sc around making a long st down into rnd 2 bet each flower petal. End with sl st in first ch of rnd and fasten off.

Round 5: Change color. Ch 3, 3 dc, ch 1, *dc in same st as last dc, 3 dc, ch 1 (sk long st of the prev rnd), 4 dc, ch 1; rep from * 5 times, dc in same st as last dc, 3 dc, ch 1, sl st in top ch of the beg ch 3. Fasten off.

Tip: African flower motifs make beautiful afghans when joined together.

Cluster Cross

Stitches Used

Chain stitch (ch), **cluster** (CL), **double crochet** (dc), **slip stitch** (sl st)

Instructions

Ch 8, join with sl st in first ch to form ring.

Round 1: Ch 3 (counts as first dc), beg CL in ring, *ch 5, 1 CL in ring, ch 2 **, 1 CL in ring; rep from * twice; rep from * to ** once, join with sl st in top ch of beg ch 3.

Round 2: Sl st to center of next ch-5 sp, ch 3 (counts as first dc), beg CL in first sp, *ch 2, 3 dc in next ch-2 sp, ch 2 **, (1 CL, ch 2, 1 CL) in next ch-5 sp; rep from * twice; rep from * to ** once, 1 CL in same ch-5 sp as beg CL, ch 1, sl st in top ch of beg ch 3.

Round 3: Ch 3 (counts as first dc), beg CL in first sp, *ch 2, work 2 dc in next ch-2 sp, 1 dc in each of the next 3 dc, 2 dc in next ch-2 sp, ch 2 **, (1 CL, ch 2, 1 CL) in next ch-2 sp; rep from * twice; rep from * to ** once, 1 CL in same sp as beg CL, ch 1, sl st in top ch of beg ch 3.

Round 4: Ch 3 (counts as first dc), beg CL in first sp, *ch 2, 2 dc in next ch-2 sp, 1 dc in each of the next 7 dc, 2 dc in next ch-2 sp, ch 2 **, (1 CL, ch 3, 1 CL) in next ch-2 sp; rep from * twice; rep from * to ** once, 1 CL in same ch-2 sp as beg CL, ch 3, join with sl st in top ch of beg ch 3, fasten off.

Tip: How to make the cluster (CL)

This double crochet cluster is 3 dc sts joined together. Leave the last lp of each dc on the hook and then yo and draw yarn through all 4 remaining lps on hook to complete. Beg cluster uses starting ch 3 + 2 dc.

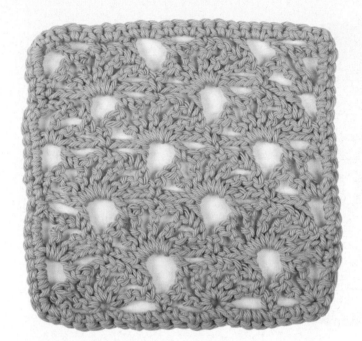

Open Fan

Stitches Used

Chain stitch (ch), **double crochet** (dc), **fan stitch**, **single crochet** (sc), **treble crochet** (tr)

Instructions

Ch 26 (or a multiple of 10 sts + 6).

Row 1: 1 sc in 2nd ch from hook, *ch 1, sk 4 ch, work a fan in next ch, then ch 1, sk 4 ch, 1 sc in next ch; rep from * to last 5 ch, ch 1, sk 4 ch, work [1 tr, ch 2] twice and 1 tr in last ch. Ch 1, turn.

Row 2: 1 sc in first st, *ch 3, sk next ch-2 sp, 1 dc in next sp **, ch 2, sk next tr, sc, and tr and work 1 dc in first ch-2 sp of next fan, ch 3, work 1 sc in center tr of fan, rep from * , ending last rep at **, ch 1, 1 tr in last sc. Ch 7, turn.

Row 3: Sk first tr, work [1 tr, ch 2, 1 tr] in next ch-1 sp, ch 1, sk next ch-3 sp, 1 sc in next sc, *ch 1, sk next ch-3 sp, work a fan in next ch-2 sp, ch 1, sk next ch-3 sp, 1 sc in next sc; rep from * to end of row. Ch 6, turn.

Row 4: Sk first tr, work 1 dc in next ch-2 sp, ch 3, 1 sc in center tr of fan, *ch 3, sk next ch-2 sp, 1 dc in next ch-2 sp, ch 2, sk next tr, sc, and tr; work 1 dc in next ch-2 sp, ch 3, 1 sc in center tr of fan; rep from * , ending last rep in 3rd ch of beg ch 6. Ch 1, turn.

Row 5: *1 sc in sc, ch 1, sk next ch-3 sp, fan in next ch-2 sp, ch 1, sk next ch-3 sp; rep from * to last sc, 1 sc in sc, ch 1, sk next ch-3 sp, work [1 tr, ch 2] twice and 1 tr in last st.

Rep rows 2–5 until desired size.

Edging (optional):

Add a row of sc to edge square.

Tip: **How to make the fan stitch**

To make this fan stitch, work 1 tr, [ch 2, 1 tr] 4 times.

Circle Lace Square

Stitches Used

Chain stitch (ch), **double crochet** (dc), **half double crochet** (hdc), **single crochet** (sc), **slip stitch** (sl st), **treble crochet** (tr)

Instructions

Make a magic circle.

Round 1: Ch 3, work 19 dc in circle, pull tail to tighten circle and join with sl st in top ch of beg ch 3.

Round 2: Ch 4, *dc in next st, ch 1; rep from * around. Join with sl st in 3rd ch of beg ch 4.

Round 3: Sl st in next ch-1 sp, ch 1, sc in same sp, *ch 3, sc in next ch-3 sp; rep from * around. Join with sl st in first sc.

Round 4: Sl st in next ch-3 sp, ch 1, sc in same sp, *ch 3, sc in next ch-1 sp; rep from * around. Join with sl st in first sc.

Round 5: Rep rnd 4.

Round 6: Sl st in next ch-sp, ch 1, sc in same sp, *ch 4, sc in next ch-sp; rep from * around. Join with sl st in first sc.

Round 7: Rep rnd 6.

Round 8: Sl st in next ch-sp, ch 1, sc in same sp, *ch 5, sc in next ch-sp; rep from * around. Join with sl st in first sc.

Round 9: Sl st in next ch-sp, ch 4, work 6 tr in same ch-sp, 4 dc in next ch-sp, hdc in next sc, 3 sc in next ch-sp, sc in next sc, 3 sc in next ch-sp, hdc in next sc, 4 dc in next ch-sp, *7 tr in next ch-sp, 4 dc in next ch-sp, hdc in next sc, 3 sc in next ch-sp, sc in next sc, 3 sc in next ch-sp, hdc in next sc, 4 dc in next ch-sp; rep from * around. Join with sl st in 3rd ch of beg ch 4.

Round 10: Sl st in next st, ch 4, sk 1 st, work 7 dc in next st, ch 1, *(sk 1 st, dc in next st, ch 1), rep to next corner, 7 dc in corner st; rep from * around. Join with sl st in 3rd ch of beg ch 4.

Round 11: Ch 3, dc in next 4 sts, 5 dc in next st, dc in next 29 sts, 5 dc in next st, dc in next 29 sts, 5 dc in next st, dc in next 29 sts, 5 dc in next st, dc in next 24 sts, join with sl st in top ch of beg ch 3. Fasten off.

Hexagon

Stitches Used

Chain stitch (ch), **cluster** (CL),
double crochet (dc), **slip stitch** (sl st)

Instructions

Ch 5, join with sl st in first ch to form ring.

Round 1: Ch 3, beg CL in ring, ch 2, *1 CL, ch 2 in ring; rep from * 5 times, join with sl st in top of first CL. Fasten off.

Round 2: Change color and draw yarn through next ch-2 sp, ch 3, beg CL, ch 2, *(1 CL, ch 2, 1 CL, ch 2) in next sp; rep from * 4 more times, join with sl st in top of first CL and fasten off.

Round 3: Change color and draw yarn through next ch-2 sp, ch 3, 2 dc in same sp, *(3 dc, ch 2, 3 dc) in next ch-2 sp, 3 dc in next ch-sp; rep from * 4 more times, (3 dc, ch 2, 3 dc) in final ch-2 sp, join with sl st in top ch of first ch 3 and fasten off.

Tip: **How to make the cluster (CL)**

To make this double crochet cluster, yo and draw a loop through, yo and draw through 2 loops (3 times), yo and draw through remaining 4 loops on hook to finish. Beg cluster uses starting ch 3 + 2 dc.

Circles in a Square

Stitches Used

Chain stitch (ch), **double crochet** (dc), **double treble crochet** (dtr), **half double crochet** (hdc), **single crochet** (sc), **slip stitch** (sl st), **treble crochet** (tr)

Instructions

Using color A, make a magic circle.

Round 1: Ch 3 (counts as first dc), 11 dc in circle and pull beg tail to tighten. Join with sl st in top of beg ch 3.

Round 2: Ch 3 (counts as first dc), 1 dc in joining st, *2 dc in next st; rep from * around, join with sl st in top of beg ch 3.

Round 3: Ch 3 (counts as first dc), 1 dc in joining st, 1 dc in next stitch, *2 dc in next st, 1 dc in next st; rep from * around, join with sl st in top of beg ch 3.

Round 4: Using color B, ch 3 (counts as first dc), 1 dc in joining st, 1 dc in next 2 sts, *2 dc in next st, dc in next 2 sts; rep from * around, join with sl st in top of beg ch 3.

Round 5: Ch 3 (counts as first dc), 1 dc in joining st, 1 dc in next 3 sts, *2 dc in next st, dc in next 3 sts; rep from * around, join with sl st in top of beg ch 3.

Round 6: Ch 3 (counts as first dc), 1 dc in joining st, 1 dc in next 4 sts, *2 dc in next st, dc in next 4 sts; rep from * around, join with sl st in top of beg ch 3. Fasten off.

Round 7: Using color C, join yarn in any st and ch 1 (counts as first sc), sc in next 3 sts, hdc in next 2 sts, dc in next 2 sts, tr in next 2 sts, (1 dtr, ch 1, 1 dtr) in next st, *2 tr, 2 dc, 2 hdc, 5 sc, 2 hdc, 2 dc, 2 tr, (1 dtr, ch 1, 1 dtr); rep from * twice, 2 tr, 2 dc, 2 hdc, 4 sc, join in first ch with sl st.

Round 8: Ch 3, dc in joining st, dc in next 9 sts, (2 dc, 1 tr, ch 1, 1 tr, 2 dc) in corner st, *dc in next 18 sts, (2 dc, 1 tr, ch 1, 1 tr, 2 dc) in corner st; rep from * twice, dc in the next 9 sts, join with sl st in the top of the beg ch 3. Fasten off.

Tip: How to double treble crochet (dtr)
Yo 3 times, insert hook in st, yo, draw up a lp, *yo, draw yarn through 2 lps; rep from * 3 times.

Nested Square

Instructions

Using color A, ch 26.

Base row: Using color A, 1 sc in 2nd ch from hook and in each ch to end of row. Ch 1, turn.

Rows 1–5: Using color A, 1 sc in first and each sc st to end of row. Ch 1, turn.

Rows 6–20: Work 5 sc sts in color A, 15 sc sts in color B, and 5 sc sts in color A. (This gives you a total of 25 sc sts.) **Note:** When changing to color B, work over color A instead of fastening off. Pick up color A again when switching from color B.

Rows 21–25: Rep rows 1–5.

Edging (optional):

To work a sl st edging, use the same color yarn (A) to crochet 2 rounds of sl st all the way around the square. When you work the 2nd round, be sure to work in the BL only.

Tip: Use contrasting colors for a bold nested square design or a monochromatic color scheme for a subtle design.

Catherine Wheel

Stitches Used

Chain stitch (ch), **cluster** (CL), **double crochet** (dc), **single crochet** (sc)

Instructions

Each row is worked in a different color.

Ch 26 (or a multiple of 10 sts + 6).

Row 1: 1 sc in 2nd ch from hook, 1 sc in next ch, *sk 3 ch, 7 dc in next ch, sk 3 ch, 1 sc in each of the next 3 ch; rep from * to last 4 ch, sk 3 ch, 4 dc in last ch, (change color), ch 1, turn.

Row 2: 1 sc in first st, 1 sc in next st, *ch 3, 1 CL over next 7 sts, ch 3, 1 sc in each of the next 3 sts; rep from * to last 4 sts, ch 3, 1 CL over last 4 sts, (change color), ch 3, turn.

Row 3: 3 dc in first st, *sk 3 ch, 1 sc in each of next 3 sc, sk 3 ch, 7 dc in lp that closed next CL; rep from * to end, finishing with sk 3 ch, 1 sc in each of last 2 sc, (change color), ch 3, turn.

Row 4: Sk first st, 1 CL over next 3 sts, *ch 3, 1 sc in each of next 3 sts, ch 3, 1 CL over next 7 sts; rep from * to end, finishing with ch 3, 1 sc in each of the last 2 sc sts, (change color), ch 1, turn.

Row 5: 1 sc in each of the first 2 sc, *sk 3 ch, 7 dc in lp that closed next CL, sk 3 ch, 1 sc in each of the next 3 sc; rep from * to end, finishing with sk 3 ch, 4 dc in last st. (change color).

Rep rows 2–5 until desired size.

Edging (optional):
Add fan edging to create square.

Tip: How to make the cluster (CL)
Work [yo, insert hook where instructed by pattern, yo, draw lp through, yo, draw through 2 lps] over the number of sts indicated, yo, draw through all remaining lps on hook.

Honeycomb Stitch

Stitches Used
Chain stitch (ch), **single crochet** (sc), **treble crochet** (tr)

Instructions

Ch 22 (or a multiple of 5 sts + 2).

Row 1: Work 1 sc in 2nd ch from hook, 1 sc in each ch to end of row. Ch 1, turn.

Row 2: 1 sc in each of the first 2 sc, *ch 5, sk 2 sc, 1 sc in each of next 3 sc; rep from * to end of row, omitting 1 sc at end of last rep. Ch 1, turn.

Row 3: 1 sc in first sc, *5 sc in next 5-ch arch, sk 1 sc, 1 sc in next sc; rep from * to end of row. Ch 6 (counts as 1 tr, 2 ch), turn.

Row 4: Sk first 2 sc, 1 sc in each of the next 3 sc, *ch 5, sk 3 sc, 1 sc in each of the next 3 sc; rep from * to last 2 sc, ch 2, 1 tr in last sc. Ch 1, turn.

Row 5: 1 sc in first tr, 2 sc in ch-2 sp, sk 1 sc, 1 sc in next sc, *5 sc in next 5-ch arch, sk 1 sc, 1 sc in next sc; rep from * to last ch-2 sp, 2 sc in last sp, 1 sc in 4th of ch 6 at beg of prev row. Ch 1, turn.

Row 6: 1 sc in each of first 2 sc, *ch 5, sk 3 sc, 1 sc in each of next 3 sc; rep from * to end, omitting 1 sc at end of last rep.

Rep rows 3–6 until desired size or after 18 rows. Fasten off.

Tip: How to treble crochet (tr)

Yarn over twice and insert hook, yarn over and draw through the first loop, yarn over and draw through first 2 loops, yarn over and draw through first 2 loops, yarn over and draw through both loops to complete stitch.

Irish Rose Square

Stitches Used

Chain stitch (ch), **double crochet** (dc), **half double crochet** (hdc), **shell stitch**, **single crochet** (sc), **slip stitch** (sl st)

Instructions

Flower:

Make a magic circle.

Round 1: Ch 1, 16 sc in circle, pull tail to tighten circle, sl st in first sc to join.

Round 2 (small petals): Ch 4, *sk 1 st, sl st in next st, ch 3; rep from * around. Join with sl st in first ch of beg ch 4.

Round 3 (small petals): Work (1 sc, 1 hdc, 1 dc, 1 hdc, 1 sc) in each ch-3 sp. Join with sl st in first sc.

Round 4 (medium petals): On the back of the flower, sl st around the post bet petals in prev rnd. Ch 5, sl st around post bet next 2 petals. *Ch 4, sl st around post bet next 2 petals; rep from * around. Ch 4, join with sl st in the first ch of beg ch 5.

Round 5 (medium petals): Work (1 sc, 1 hdc, 3 dc, 1 hdc, 1 sc) in each ch-4 sp. Join with sl st in the first sc.

Round 6 (large petals): On the back of the flower, sl st around the post bet petals in prev rnd. Ch 6, sl st around post bet next 2 petals. *Ch 5, sl st around post bet next 2 petals; rep from * around; ch 5, join with sl st in the first ch of beg ch 6.

Round 7 (large petals): Work (1 sc, 1 hdc, 5 dc, 1 hdc, 1 sc) in each ch-5 sp around. Join with sl st in first sc.

Round 8: On the back of the flower, sl st around the post bet petals in prev rnd. Ch 6, sl st around post bet next 2 petals. *Ch 5, sl st around post bet next 2 petals; rep from * around. Ch 5, join with sl st in the top ch of beg ch 6. Fasten off.

Rounds 9–12: Continued on next page.

Square: Change color.

Round 9: With new color, join with sl st to the middle of any ch-6 sp. Ch 3, 2 dc in same sp. *Ch 2, (2 dc, ch 2) twice in next ch-6 sp. Work shell st in next ch-6 sp; rep from * 3 times. Ch 2, (2 dc, ch 2) twice in next ch-6 sp, 3 dc in next ch-6 sp, ch 2. Join with sl st in the top of beg ch 3.

Round 10: Ch 3, 2 dc in same sp. *Ch 2, dc in last dc of shell st. Ch 2, dc in next dc, sk next dc, 2 dc in ch-2 sp, sk next dc, dc in next dc, ch 2. Dc in first dc of next shell st, ch 2, shell st in ch-2 sp of shell; rep from * 3 times. Ch 2, dc in last dc of shell, ch 2, dc in next dc, sk next dc, 2 dc in ch-2 sp, sk next dc, dc in next dc. Ch 2, dc in first dc of next shell st, ch 2, 3 dc in ch-2 sp of shell st, ch 2, join with sl st in top of beg ch 3.

Round 11: Ch 3, 2 dc in same sp. *Ch 2, dc in last dc of shell st. Ch 2, **dc in next dc, 2 dc in ch-2 sp, dc in next dc, ch 2** sk next 2 dc; rep from ** to **. Dc in first dc of next shell st, ch 2, shell st in ch-2 sp of shell st; rep from * 3 times. Ch 2, dc in last dc of next shell st, ch 2, *dc in next dc, 2 dc in ch-2 sp, dc in next dc*; sk next 2 dc; rep from * to *. Ch 2, dc in first dc of next shell st, ch 2, 3 dc in ch-2 sp of shell st, ch 2. Join with sl st in the top of beg ch 3.

Round 12: Ch 1, sc in each st around, working 1 sc in each ch-2 sp and 3 sc in each corner. Join with sl st in the first sc. Fasten off.

𝒯ip: **How to make the shell stitch**
In the next space, work (3 dc, ch 2, 3 dc).

Woven Stitch

Stitches Used
Chain stitch (ch), **single crochet** (sc)

Instructions

Ch an even number of sts.

Row 1: Sc in 2nd ch from hook, *ch 1, sk 1 ch, 1 sc in next ch; rep from * to end, turn.

Row 2: Ch 1, sk first sc, *1 sc in ch-1 sp, ch 1, sk 1 sc; rep from *, ending with 1 sc in ch 1, turn.

Rep row 2 until desired size.

Moon Square

Stitches Used

Chain stitch (ch), **cluster** (CL), **double crochet** (dc), **single crochet** (sc), **slip stitch** (sl st), **treble crochet** (tr)

Instructions

Using color A, ch 6, join with sl st in first ch to form a ring.

Round 1: Ch 3 (counts as first dc), 2 dc in ring, *3 dc in ring, ch 2; rep from * 3 times in ring, joining with sl st in top ch of beg ch 3.

Round 2: Sl st in first sp, ch 3 (counts as first dc), beg CL in sp, ch 6, CL, *ch 3, (1 CL, ch 6, 1 CL), in next sp; rep from * 3 times, join color B in top ch of beg ch 3.

Round 3: Sl st in first sp, ch 3, (3 dc, ch 3, 4 dc) in sp, ch 1, 2 dc in middle dc of 3-dc group in first rnd, ch 1, *(4 dc, ch 3, 4 dc) in sp, ch 1, 2 dc in middle dc of 3-dc group below in first rnd, ch 1; rep from * 3 times, sl st in top ch of beg ch 3, fasten off.

Round 4: Join color A in a corner sp, ch 3, (2 dc, ch 3, 3 dc) in sp, ch 3, 2 tr in ch-3 sp of 2nd rnd below, 2 tr on other side of same ch-3 sp of 2nd rnd below, ch 3, *(3 dc, ch 3, 3 dc) in next corner sp, ch 3, 2 tr in ch-3 sp of 2nd rnd below, 2 tr on other side of same ch-3 sp of 2nd rnd below, ch 3; rep from * 3 times, join with sl st in top ch of beg ch 3.

Round 5: Sl st in sp, ch 3 (1 dc, ch 2, 2 dc) in corner sp, *[dc in next dc] 3 times, 3 dc in next sp, [dc in next tr] twice, 2 dc in next sp, [dc in next tr] twice, 3 dc in next sp [dc in next dc] 3 times, [2 dc, ch 2, 2 dc] in corner sp; rep from * 3 times, [dc in next dc] 3 times, 3 dc in next sp, [dc in next tr] twice, 2 dc in next sp, [dc in next tr] twice, 3 dc in next sp, [dc in next dc] 3 times, join color B in top ch of beg ch 3.

Round 6: Sc in each dc, making 3 sc in each corner sp. Fasten off.

Tip: How to make the cluster (CL)

Use 3 dc joined together. Leave the last lp of each dc on hook, then yo and draw through all remaining 4 lps on hook to complete. Beg cluster uses starting ch 3 + 2 dc.

Projects

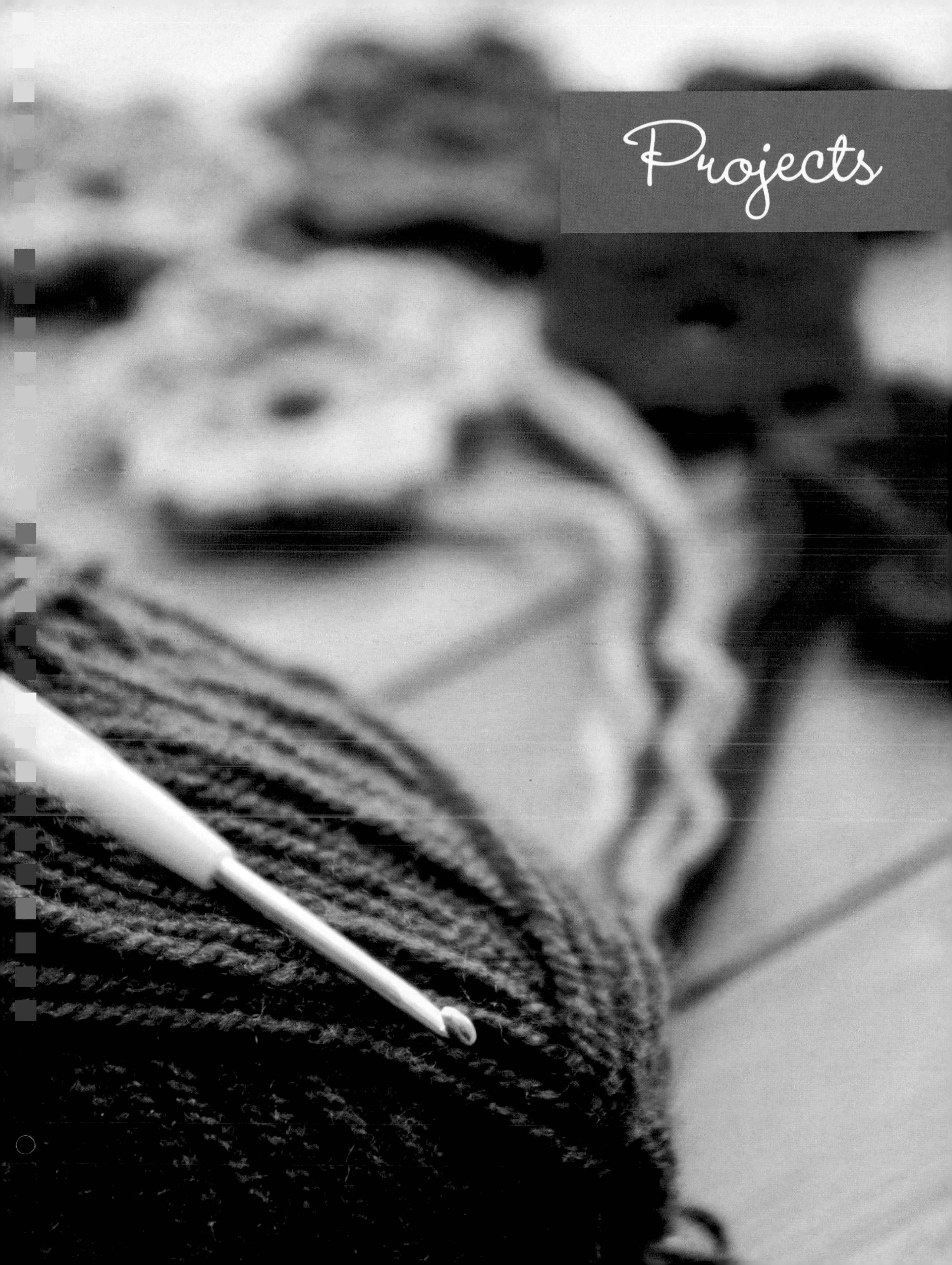

Mug Cozy

Skill Level

EASY

Materials

MEDIUM
4

Hook: 4.5 mm/U.S. 7
Other: 1 button, pin, yarn needle

Stitches Used

Chain stitch (ch)
Double crochet (dc)
Half double crochet (hdc)
Single crochet (sc)
Slip stitch (sl st)

Instructions

Ch 8.

Row 1: 1 sc and 1 dc in 2nd ch from hook, *sk next ch, 1 sc and 1 dc in next ch; rep from * to end of row, ch 1, turn.

Row 2: *Sk next st, 1 sc and 1 dc in next st; rep from * to end of row, ch 1, turn.

Rep row 2 until work measures 8 in. from beg.

Next row: Sk first st, sl st in the next 2 sts, 1 hdc in each of the next 4 sts, ch 1, turn.

You will now be working on these 4 sts to make buttonhole strip.

Next row: 1 hdc in each st, ch 1, turn.

Rep last row until buttonhole strip measures 2 in.

Next row: 1 hdc in first st, ch 2 and sk next 2 sts, 1 hdc in last st.

Work sc border evenly around, working 3 sc in corners and 2 sc in ch-2 buttonhole sp. Join with sl st in first sc.

Finishing

Fasten off and weave in ends.

Attach the button.

Tip: Attaching the button

1. Wrap your cozy around your mug so you can see where you want the button to go. Mark it with a pin.
2. Thread a yarn needle with a piece of yarn about 7 in.
3. Place your button where you have marked with a pin. Remove the pin and hold the button in place.
4. Insert the needle from back to front through 1 buttonhole. (Leave about a 2 in. tail on the back side.)
   Insert the needle through the next hole from the front. Repeat until you feel the button is secure.
5. Make a knot with the 2 tails that are left and cut the excess yarn.

Toy Ball

Skill Level

EASY

Materials

MEDIUM
4

Hook: 4.5 mm/U.S. 7
Other: Polyfill stuffing, stitch marker, yarn needle

Stitches Used

Chain stitch (ch)
Single crochet (sc)
Single crochet decrease
Slip stitch (sl st)
Treble crochet (tr)

Tip: Single crochet decrease
Insert hook through next st, yo, draw through, leaving 2 lps on hook, insert hook in next st, yo, draw through, leaving 3 lps on hook, yo and draw through all 3 lps.

Tip: Change colors as often as you would like to create a unique pattern.

Instructions

All rnds will be worked continuously. Use a stitch marker at the beg of each rnd.

Make a magic circle.

Round 1: 9 sc in circle.

Round 2: 2 sc in each st around.

Round 3: 1 sc in each st around.

Round 4: *1 sc in each of the next 2 sts, 2 sc in next st; rep from * around.

Round 5: *1 sc in each of the next 3 sts, 2 sc in next st; rep from * around.

Round 6: *1 sc in each of the next 4 sts, 2 sc in next st; rep from * around.

Rounds 7–12: 1 sc in each st around.

Round 13: *1 sc in each of the next 4 sts, sc decrease; rep from * around.

Round 14: *1 sc in each of the next 3 sts, sc decrease; rep from * around.

Round 15: *1 sc in each of the next 2 sts, sc decrease; rep from * around.

Round 16: 1 sc in each st around.

Stuff ball generously with polyfill stuffing. The ball needs more stuffing than you might think.

Round 17: Sc decrease around.

Round 18: Sl st, sk 1 st, sl st around. Fasten off, leaving a long tail to sew ball closed.

Finishing

Step 1: With a threaded yarn needle, stitch back and forth in different directions to close up the hole.

Step 2: Once the hole is completed closed, secure and sew the top tightly.

Step 3: Use your hands to shape ball and make sure the stuffing is evenly distributed.

Tip: Before closing the ball, try adding catnip or a small bell to make a fun toy for your favorite furry friend!

Infinity Scarf

Skill Level

BEGINNER

Materials

MEDIUM **4** 3 skeins

Hook: 5.5 mm/U.S. I-9
Other: Yarn needle

Stitches Used

Chain stitch (ch)
Double crochet (dc)
Treble crochet (tr)
Whipstitch

Instructions

Ch 36.

Row 1: Tr in 7th and 8th ch from hook. Dc behind first tr in 6th ch. *Sk 1 ch (from the 2nd tr). Tr in next 2 ch. Dc in the skipped ch. Rep from * 8 more times (only 1 ch is left unworked). Tr in last ch.

Row 2: Ch 4, turn. *Sk next st. Tr in next 2 sts. Dc in skipped st. Rep from * 9 more times. Tr in last st.

Rep row 2 until desired length. This example is 28 inches long when both ends are joined.

Finishing

Join both ends with a whipstitch.

Tip: Using a variegated yarn is a great choice for making scarves. It gives you color variety without having to change colors during your project.

Tip: Joining with a whipstitch

Hold both ends of the scarf together with stitches and rows lined up. Start on the right. Insert the threaded yarn needle from back to front through the first stitch on both ends. Take the needle over the top of both ends and insert it from back to front through the next pair of stitches on the left. Repeat until you reach the end of the seam. Fasten off and weave in yarn tails.

whipstitch seam

Afghan

Skill Level

EASY

Materials

SUPER BULKY
 8 skeins

Hook: 9 mm/U.S. M–13

Stitches Used

Chain stitch (ch)
Double crochet (dc)
Single crochet (sc)
Slip stitch (sl st)

Tip: Yarn is colored in batches and given a dye lot number. Color may vary slightly from batch to batch. Make sure to buy enough yarn at the start of your project, all from the same dye lot, so that the color is consistent throughout.

Instructions

Ch 61 (or to desired width, odd number of ch sts).

Row 1: Dc in 5th ch from hook, ch 1, dc in same ch (v-stitch made), *sk 2 ch, (1 dc, ch 1, 1 dc) in next ch (v-stitch made); rep from * to last 2 ch, sk 1 ch, dc in last ch.

Rows 2–40 (or desired length): Ch 3, turn, (1 dc, ch 1, 1 dc) in each ch-1 sp across, dc in top of tch. Fasten off.

Edging

Join yarn in any corner of afghan.

Edging row 1: Ch 1, sc evenly spaced along all edges of afghan with 3 sc in each corner. Sl st with first st to end row.

Edging row 2: Ch 3, dc in each sc around all edges of afghan with (1 dc, ch 1, 1 dc) in each corner sc. Sl st with first st to end row.

Edging row 3: Rep edging row 2. Fasten off and weave in yarn tails.

Ice Pop Cozies

Skill Level

BEGINNER

Materials

MEDIUM
4

Hook: 4.5 mm/U.S. 7
Other: Stitch markers

Stitches Used

Chain stitch (ch)
Half double crochet (hdc)
Slip stitch (sl st)

Instructions

Ch 13, sl st in first ch to create ring.

Round 1: Ch 2, 13 hdc in ring, sl st in top of ch 2 to close. Work each round continuously; use stitch markers if necessary to keep track of rnds.

Round 2: 13 hdc around.

Round 3: 13 hdc around.

Round 4: Change color, 13 hdc around.

Round 5: 13 hdc around.

Round 6: 13 hdc around.

Round 7: Change color, 13 hdc around.

Round 8: 13 hdc around.

Round 9: 13 hdc around, sl st to close.

Rep to make additional cozies.

Heart Bookmark

Skill Level

EASY

Materials

Hook: 4.5 mm/U.S. 7

Stitches Used

Chain stitch (ch)
Double crochet (dc)
Large picot
Slip stitch (sl st)
Small picot
Treble crochet (tr)

Instructions

Heart

Make a magic circle.

Round 1: Ch 4, 2 tr in circle, 3 dc in circle, ch 1, 1 tr, ch 1, 3 dc, 3 tr, ch 3 and join with sl st in center of heart (magic circle); pull tail of magic circle to tighten heart.

Stem

Attach a 2nd color yarn with sl st in the center of heart, ch 42 (or as long as you like), sl st in 6th ch from hook, *sl st in next 6 ch sts, small picot, sl st in next 6 ch sts, large picot; rep from * 2 times, sl st in end of ch and fasten off.

Tip: **How to make the picot stitch**

For small picot: Ch 3, insert hook in 3rd ch from hook, yo, and draw through both lps.

For large picot: Ch 5, insert hook in 5th ch from hook, yo, and draw through both lps.

Slouch Hat

Skill Level

EASY

Materials

2 skeins

Hook: 4.5 mm/U.S. 7

Other: Yarn needle

Stitches Used

Chain stitch (ch)

Front loops (FL)

Puff stitch

Single crochet (sc)

Slip stitch (sl st)

Instructions

Hat band

Ch 11.

Row 1: Sc in 2nd ch from hook and in each ch to end of row.

Row 2: Ch 2, turn. Sc in FL only across row.

Rows 3 and on: Rep row 2. Cont with the sc FL only rows until the band measures about 22 in., or to fit comfortably around your head. Fasten off, leaving a tail to sew ends of band together. Use a yarn needle to sew ends of band together to create a circle.

Hat body

Make a slip knot and push hook through first sc where the band was sewn up. Ch 1, sc all around band. Join with sl st in first ch.

Round 1: Ch 2, *puff st, ch 1, sk 1 st; rep from * around.

Round 2: Working around continuously, work *puff st in ch-1 sp from prev rnd, ch 1, sk 1 st; rep from * around.

Rounds 3–20 (or desired size of hat): Rep rnd 2.

Finishing

Seam it up.

Don't connect last rnd. Insert hook in front of hat and sc to connect. It will make a figure 8 shape. Turn hat, insert hook in center side of hat, and sc to connect. Turn hat, insert hook in center side of hat, and sc to connect. It will now have a star shape. Cont turning and sc to connect until the top of hat is closed enough to your liking. Fasten off and weave in yarn tails.

Tip: **How to make the puff stitch**

To make the puff stitch, yarn over and insert your hook in the stitch, yarn over and draw the loop through, [yarn over and insert your hook into the same place] repeat until there are 7 loops on your hook. Yarn over and draw the yarn through all 7 loops.

Potholder

Skill Level

■■■□
INTERMEDIATE

Materials

MEDIUM
4

Hook: 4.5 mm/U.S. 7
Other: Stitch markers, yarn needle

Stitches Used

Chain stitch (ch)
Double crochet (dc)
Seed stitch
Single crochet (sc)
Slip stitch (sl st)

Instructions

Ch 27.

Round 1: Ch 1, 1 sc in 2nd ch from hook, 1 dc in next ch. *1 sc in next ch, 1 dc in next ch; rep from * around, working both sides of foundation ch. Join with sl st in first sc to complete rnd.

Mark the beg st of a rnd with a stitch marker so you know where the rnd ends.

Rounds 2–12: 1 seed st in each dc of the prev rnd. Join with sl st in beg sc (of seed st). Turn your work so the opposite side faces you.

Finishing

The piece will be in the shape of a pouch with an opening at the top. Lay the piece down so that you have a square. Fold the opening edges so they come together and touch each other. This will form 2 more points on the potholder, creating the square. Sew seam shut with a needle, fasten off and sew in all yarn tails.

Tip: **How to make the seed stitch**
The seed stitch used to make this potholder is a combination of 1 single crochet and 1 double crochet worked into the same chain or stitch.

sewn seam

Baby Blanket

Skill Level

EASY

Materials

 8 skeins

Hook: 6.5 mm/U.S. K-10.5

Stitches Used

Chain stitch (ch)
Double crochet (dc)
Double crochet 3 together (dc3tog)
Slip stitch (sl st)

Tip: Double crochet 3 together (dc3tog)

1. Yarn over. Insert your hook into the stitch.

2. Yarn over and draw the yarn through the stitch.

3. Yarn over and draw the yarn through the first 2 loops on your hook.

4. Repeat steps 1–3 two times, inserting your hook into the same stitch. You will have 4 loops on your hook.

5. Yarn over and draw through all 4 loops on your hook. There will be 1 loop left when dc3tog is complete.

Instructions

Ch 141.

Row 1: Dc in 4th st from hook, *dc in next 5 sts, dc3tog, dc in next 5 sts, (1 dc, ch 1, 1 dc) in next st; rep from * 10 times, ending with 2 dc in the final st.

Row 2: Ch 3, turn. Dc in first st. *Dc in next 5 sts, dc3tog, dc in next 5 sts, (1 dc, ch 1, 1 dc) in next st; rep from * 10 times, ending with 2 dc in the final st.

Row 3: Ch 3, turn. Dc in first st. *Dc in next 5 sts, dc3tog, dc in next 5 sts, (1 dc, ch 1, 1 dc) in next st; rep from * 10 times, ending with 2 dc in the final st.

Row 4: Change color. Ch 3, turn. Dc in first st. *Dc in next 5 sts, dc3tog, dc in next 5 sts, (1 dc, ch 1, 1 dc) in next st; rep from * 10 times, ending with 2 dc in the final st.

Row 5: Ch 3, turn. Dc in first st. *Dc in next 5 sts, dc3tog, dc in next 5 sts, (1 dc, ch 1, 1 dc) in next st; rep from * 10 times, ending with 2 dc in the final st.

Row 6: Ch 3, turn. Dc in first st. *Dc in next 5 sts, dc3tog, dc in next 5 sts, (1 dc, ch 1, 1 dc) in next st; rep from * 10 times, ending with 2 dc in the final st.

Row 7: Change color. Ch 3, turn. Dc in first st. *Dc in next 5 sts, dc3tog, dc in next 5 sts, (1 dc, ch 1, 1 dc) in next st; rep from * 10 times, ending with 2 dc in the final st.

Rows 8 and on: Rep rows 2–7 until desired size. Make sure to end final 3 rows with the same color you started with. Fasten off.

Edging

Join your starting color to first raw edge of blanket and work a single row of dc evenly. Sl st to close and fasten off. Join your starting color to 2nd raw edge of blanket and work a single row of dc evenly. Sl st to close and fasten off.

Table Centerpiece

Skill Level

INTERMEDIATE

Materials

 2 skeins (1 of each color)

Hook: 4.5 mm/U.S. 7

Stitches Used

Back loops (BL)
Chain stitch (ch)
Double crochet (dc)
Front loops (FL)
Picot stitch
Single crochet (sc)
Slip stitch (sl st)

Tip: Work rows 7–9 and 25–27 in the edging color, or a new color, to add a pop of color.

Instructions

Ch 38.

Work all sc sts in FL unless directed otherwise.

Row 1: Working in FL only, sc in 3rd ch from hook and in every ch afterward.

Rows 2–6: Ch 2, turn. Work entire row in sc.

Row 7: Ch 3, turn. 1 dc in next st. Sk next 2 sts. *(1 dc, ch 1, 1 dc) in following st, sk 2 sts; rep from * 11 times total. Work 1 more dc in each of the last 2 sts.

Row 8: Ch 3, turn. 1 dc in next st. Working in ch-1 sps, *(1 dc, ch 1, 1 dc) in each sp; rep from * 11 times total. Work 2 more dc to end row.

Row 9: Ch 2, turn. Sc in first dc st from prev row. Working in the sps from prev row, 1 sc in each sp bet dc sts, and 2 sc in each ch-1 sp. At the end of the row, sc in the last dc and last ch of tch.

Rows 10–24: Ch 2, turn. Work entire row in sc.

Row 25: Rep row 7.

Row 26: Rep row 8.

Row 27: Rep row 9.

Rows 28–32: Ch 2, turn. Work entire row in sc.

Edging

Work in BL of sts unless directed otherwise.

Round 1: Ch 2. Work sc sts across the top edge of the work, making sure to space them evenly. (1 sc, ch 2, 1 sc) in each corner and cont working around.

Round 2: Ch 2, sc in next sc, ch 1, sk 1 sc, sc in following sc st, *(ch 1, sk next sc, sc in following sc) until end of row, ch 1 (1 sc, ch 2, 1 sc) in corner sp. Rep from * around, sl st to join in beg of rnd.

Round 3: Ch 3, sk next sc, sc in the sp formed by the ch st in prev row, *(ch 1, sk next sc, sc in sp from prev row), ch 1, (1 sc, ch 2, 1 sc) in corner sp. Rep from * around, sc in same ch-2 corner sp that last sc was worked. Ch 1, sl st to join work in beg of rnd.

Round 4: Ch 3, sc in sp below, *(ch 1, sk next sc, sc in sp below) until end of row, ch 1 (1 sc, ch 2, 1 sc) in corner sp. Rep from * around. Sc in same ch-2 corner sp that last sc st was worked. Ch 1, 1 sc, ch 1, sl st to join work in beg of rnd.

Round 5: (Work all dc sts in the ch-1 sps formed in the prev row.) Ch 3, dc, skipping next sc, insert hook in next ch-1 sp, ch 1, dc in same ch-1 sp as prev dc. *(Ch 1, dc skipping next ch-1 sp and inserting hook in following ch-1 sp. Ch 1, dc in same ch-1 sp as prev dc) rep until end, ch 1, dc in ch corner sp, ch 3 to form corner; rep from * around. Dc in same ch-2 corner sp, ch 2, dc in the sl st at the base of the first 3 ch sts that began the rnd. Ch 1, sl st to 3rd ch to join.

Round 6: (Work all sc sts in ch-1 sps from prev row.) Ch 2, *(sc in ch-1 sp, ch 3, sl st in first ch to form picot. Sc in same ch-1 sp, sc in next ch-1 sp); rep from * until end of row, (2 sc, ch 1, 1 dc, ch 1, 2 sc) in corner sp; rep from * around. Sc in next ch-1 sp. Sc in next ch-1 sp bet dc sts. Ch 3, sl st to first ch to form picot, sc in same ch-1 sp. Sl st to join in beg of rnd. Fasten off.

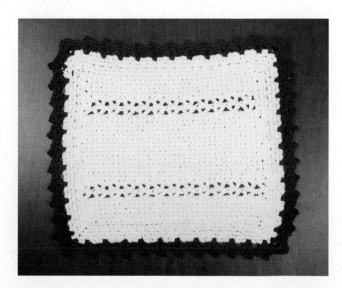

Flower Pin

Step 1: Loosely arrange the layers to form a flower.

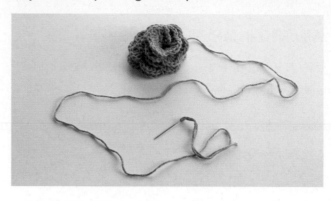

Skill Level

EASY

Materials

MEDIUM
4

Hook: 4.5 mm/U.S. 7
Other: 1 pin back, yarn needle

Stitches Used

Chain stitch (ch)
Double crochet (dc)
Single crochet (sc)

Step 2: Using a threaded yarn needle, stitch each layer of the flower together, ending on the back side.

Instructions

Flower

Ch 53.

Row 1: Dc in 3rd ch from hook. Dc in every following ch across row.

Row 2: Ch 1, turn. *Sc in next sp, 5 dc in next sp; rep from * to end of row. Fasten off, leaving a long tail with which to sew the flower together.

Step 3: Draw the threaded needle through the pin back. Secure the pin back onto the back of your flower and cut the excess yarn to complete the flower pin.

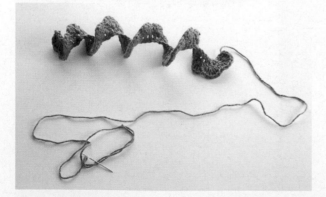

Tip: You can add crocheted flowers to scarves, headbands, necklaces, blankets, bags, or booties. The possibilities are endless!

Octopus

Skill Level

INTERMEDIATE

Materials

MEDIUM
4

Hook: 4.5 mm / U.S. 7

Other: Polyfill stuffing, safety eyes, stitch marker, yarn needle

Stitches Used

Chain stitch (ch)
Single crochet (sc)
Single crochet 2 together (sc2tog)
Slip stitch (sl st)
Treble crochet (tr)

Tip: If intended for a small child, try attaching crocheted or felt eyes.

Instructions

Body

Make a magic circle.

Round 1: Work 6 sc in magic circle. Place a marker to indicate beg of rnd, move marker up as each rnd is completed.

Round 2: 2 sc in each sc around.

Round 3: *2 sc in next sc, sc in next sc; rep from * around.

Round 4: *2 sc in next sc, sc in next 2 sc; rep from * around.

Round 5: *2 sc in next sc, sc in next 3 sc; rep from * around.

Round 6: *2 sc in next sc, sc in next 4 sc; rep from * around.

Round 7: *2 sc in next sc, sc in next 5 sc; rep from * around.

Rounds 8–17: Sc in each sc around.

Round 18: *Sc2tog, sc in next 5 sc; rep from * around.

Round 19: *Sc2tog, sc in next 4 sc; rep from * around.

Round 20: *Sc2tog, sc in next 3 sc; rep from * around.

Round 21: *Sc2tog, sc in next 2 sc; rep from * around.

Attach safety eyes and stuff generously with polyfill stuffing.

Round 22: *Sc2tog, sc in next sc; rep from * around.

Round 23: Sc2tog around.

Fasten off, leaving a long tail.

Tentacles

Make a magic circle.

Round 1: Work 8 sc in magic circle. Join with sl st in beg sc.

Round 2: Ch 18.

Round 3: Tr in 4th ch from hook, *3 tr in each ch; rep from * around until last 2 ch sts, 1 tr each in last 2 ch sts, sl st in next sc in circle.

Rep rnds 2–3 seven more times to make 8 tentacles.

Assembly

Sew the tentacle piece to the bottom of the body using the long tail left from the body. Fasten off and weave in ends.

Coasters

Skill Level

EASY

Materials

MEDIUM
4

Hook: 4.5 mm/U.S. 7

Stitches Used

Chain stitch (ch)
Decorative chain
Double crochet (dc)
Slip stitch (sl st)

Instructions

Make a magic circle.

Round 1: Ch 3 (counts as first dc), work 11 dc in circle. Pull tail of magic circle to tighten and close the circle. Sl st in top ch of the beg ch 3.

Round 2: Ch 3 (counts as first dc), work dc in same st, work 2 dc in each st around. Join with sl st in the top ch of beg ch 3.

Rep row 2 until work measures 8 in. from beg.

Round 3: Ch 3 (counts as first dc), work 2 dc in next st, *dc in next st, 2 dc in next st; rep from * around. Join with sl st in top ch of beg ch 3.

Round 4: Ch 3 (counts as first dc), *1 dc in next 2 sts, 2 dc in next st; rep from * around. Join with sl st in top ch of beg ch 3 and fasten off.

Contrast swirl (decorative chain)

Using a different color yarn, insert your hook near the center of the circle bet one of the dc from rnd 1 and pull up a lp. Insert hook bet the next 2 sts and pull up another lp. Cont around in the same manner, creating a spiral until end of the 4th rnd. Fasten off and weave in ends.

Rep to make additional coasters.

Baby Booties

Skill Level

INTERMEDIATE

Materials

MEDIUM 4

Hook: 4.5 mm/U.S. 7
Other: 2 buttons, needle, thread

Stitches Used

Chain stitch (ch)
Double crochet (dc)
Double crochet 2 together (dc2tog)
Half double crochet (hdc)
Single crochet (sc)
Single crochet 2 together (sc2tog)
Slip stitch (sl st)

Tip: These baby booties make a great keepsake gift for any newborn. Experiment with different types of yarn to make the perfect pair!

Instructions

0-3 months sizing. (Using a larger hook will create a slightly larger bootie.)

Booties will be worked in continuous rounds.

Ch 9.

Round 1: Work 3 sc in 2nd ch from hook, sc in next 3 ch, hdc in next ch, dc in next 2 ch, 7 dc in last ch. Cont working across opposite side of foundation ch, dc in next 2 ch, hdc in next ch, sc in next 3 ch.

Round 2: Cont around, starting in top of first sc of prev rnd, 2 sc in next 3 sts, sc in next 7 sts, 2 sc in next 5 sts, sc in next 7 sts.

Round 3: [Sc in next st, 2 sc in next st] 3 times, sc in next 7 sts, [sc in next st, 2 sc in next st] 5 times, sc in next 7 sts.

Round 4: Sc all around except last st. Hdc in last st.

Round 5: 8 dc, 1 hdc, 29 sc.

Round 6: Sc2tog 1 time, 6 sc, sc2tog 1 time, 7 sc, sc2tog 7 times, 7 sc.

Round 7: 15 sc, dc2tog 4 times, 6 sc.

Round 8 right bootie: Sl st 12, ch 12, sc in 5th ch from hook, sc down ch and sl st in next st on bootie. Sl st 12. Fasten off and weave in ends.

Round 8 left bootie: Sl st 22, ch 12, sc in 5th ch from hook, sc down ch and sl st in next st on bootie. Sl st 2. Fasten off and weave in ends.

Finishing

Using a needle and thread, sew a small button on each bootie corresponding with the buttonhole on the strap.

Market Bag

Skill Level

EASY

Materials

MEDIUM 4

Hooks: 4 mm/U.S. G–6, 10 mm/U.S. N–15
Other: Stitch markers

Stitches Used

Chain stitch (ch)
Double crochet (dc)
Single crochet (sc)
Slip stitch (sl st)

Instructions

Using 10 mm hook, ch 30.

Row 1: Dc in 3rd ch from hook, *(ch 1, sk 1, 1 dc); rep from * to end of row.

Row 2: Ch 1, turn work upside down and work back along the foundation chain, working bet each of the dc sts. *(1 dc, ch 1, sk 1, 1 dc); rep from * to last dc sp.

You will now beg working around rows 1 and 2.

Round 1: Ch 1, working in ch-sps of prev rnd, *(1 dc, ch 1, 1 dc); rep from * around.

Rounds 2–13: Rep rnd 1.

Round 14: Use stitch markers to mark where you would like handles to be, cont working as prev rnds until first handle marker, ch 30 for first handle, and resume working pattern until reaching 2nd handle marker, ch 30 for 2nd handle, and work pattern to end of rnd. Sl st and fasten off.

Trim

Using a 4 mm hook, work 2 sc in ch-1 sps of prev rnd until reaching handles. Work 50 sc evenly around ch sts of handles, continuing in ch-1 sps until reaching the end of rnd. Sl st and fasten off.

Headband

Skill Level

BEGINNER

Materials

Hook: 5 mm/U.S. H-8

Stitches Used

Chain stitch (ch)
Double crochet (dc)
Single crochet (sc)
Slip stitch (sl st)

Instructions

Ch 44.

Row 1: 2 dc in 3rd ch from hook, *sk 2 ch, sc in next ch, ch 2, 2 dc in same st; rep from * to end of row. Sc in last ch.

Row 2: Ch 2, turn. 2 dc in next st, *sc in ch-2 sp, ch 2, 2 dc in same sp; rep from * to end of row. Sc in top tch of prev row.

Row 3: Rep row 2.

Row 4: Rep row 2. Ch 30, sl st to the other end of the headband, creating a circle. Sl st across the short end of the headband to edge, ch 30, sl st to the other end of headband (where you started) and fasten off.

Tip: Depending on your head size, increase or decrease the number of chain stitches in row 4.

Tip: Get creative!

Try crocheting a flower embellishment to add to your headband. (Directions for the flower are on page 46.)

Pillow

Other: 1 pillow form or polyfill stuffing

Skill Level

EASY

Materials

SUPER BULKY

 3 skeins

Hook: 10 mm/U.S. N–15

Stitches Used

Back loops (BL)

Chain stitch (ch)

Double crochet (dc)

Front loops (FL)

Half double crochet (hdc)

Single crochet (sc)

Slip stitch (sl st)

Treble crochet (tr)

Instructions

Make 1 of each panel. Depending on the yarn you are using, adjust the foundation ch to fit your pillow form.

Panel 1

Ch 30.

Row 1: Sc in 3rd ch from hook and in each ch across row.

Row 2: Ch 2, turn. Work all sts in this row in FL only. Sc in first st, tr in next st. Alt sc and tr across the row, making sure to end with a sc in the last st.

Row 3: Ch 2, turn. Work in both lps for this row. Sc in each st across row.

Row 4: Ch 3, turn. Work all sts in FL only. Dc in each st across row.

Row 5: Ch 2, turn. Work all sts in FL only. Sc in each st across row.

Rep rows 2–5 five more times, or until desired size, and fasten off.

Panel 2

Ch 30.

Row 1: Sc in 3rd ch from hook and in each ch across row.

Row 2: Ch 2, turn. Work in FL only, hdc in each st across row.

Row 3: Ch 1, turn. Work in both lps, sc in each st across row.

Row 4: Ch 3, turn. Work in FL only, dc in each st across row.

Row 5: Ch 1, turn. Work in FL only, sc in each st across row.

Rep rows 2–5 until the same size as Panel 1 and fasten off.

Finishing the pillow

Hold 2 panels with wrong sides tog. Work through both thicknesses, sc evenly around to join 3 sides, working (1 sc, ch 1, 1 sc) in each corner. Once 3 sides are joined, insert pillow form or stuffing and cont closing with sc sts across. Sl st to first join and fasten off.

Arm Warmers

Skill Level

EASY

Materials

MEDIUM 4

Hook: 4.5 mm/U.S. 7

Stitches Used

Chain stitch (ch)
Double crochet (dc)
Half double crochet (hdc)
Single crochet (sc)
Slip stitch (sl st)

Instructions

Cuff

Ch 35, sl st to form ring, careful not to twist the ch.

Round 1: Ch 3, dc in next 2 ch, ch 1, sk 2 ch, *3 dc in next 3 ch, ch 1, sk 2 ch. Rep from * around, ending with ch 1 and sl st in top ch of beg ch 3.

Round 2: Ch 4 (counts as 1 dc and ch 1), *3 dc in next ch-1 sp, ch 1; rep from * around to last ch-1 sp, 2 dc in sp and sl st in 3rd ch of beg ch 4.

Round 3: Ch 3, 2 dc in ch-1 sp, ch 1, *3 dc in next ch-1 sp, ch 1; rep from * around, ending with ch 1 and sl st in top ch of beg ch 3.

Round 4: Rep rnd 2.

Round 5: Rep rnd 3.

Round 6: Ch 5, *3 dc in next ch-2 sp, ch 2; rep from * around to last ch-2 sp, 2 dc in sp and sl st in top ch of beg ch 3.

Round 7: Ch 3, 2 dc in ch-2 sp, ch 2, *3 dc in next ch-2 sp, ch 1; rep from * around, ending with ch 1 and sl st in top ch of beg ch 3.

Cont working rnds 6 and 7 until the point you'll make the thumbhole, ending with a rnd 7. The more rnds, the higher the warmers will go up your arms. 11 rnds is a nice average size.

Thumbhole

Round 1: Sl st in each of the next 2 dc and in 1 ch of first ch-2 sp of prev rnd. Ch 3, 2 dc in same ch-2 sp, *ch 2, 3 dc in next sp. Rep from * around until the last ch-2 sp of prev rnd, 1 dc in sp, ch 3, turn.

Round 2: 2 dc in ch-1 sp, ch 2, *3 dc in next ch-2 sp, ch 2. Rep from * around, ending with ch 2 and 1 dc in top ch of beg ch 3 of prev rnd.

Closing thumbhole: Ch 5, sl st in top ch of beg ch 3 of last rnd, turn.

Top round: Ch 3, 2 dc in ch-5 sp, ch 2, sk 1 dc, 3 dc in next sp, *ch 2, 3 dc in next sp. Rep from * around, ending with ch 2 and sl st in top ch of beg ch 3.

Scalloped edge

Ch 1, *5 hdc in 2nd dc of next dc group, sc in next sp. Rep from * around, ending with sl st in beg ch 1. Weave in ends.

Mini Scarf

Hook: 6 mm / U.S. J-10
Other: Yarn needle

Skill Level

INTERMEDIATE

Materials

Stitches Used

Chain stitch (ch)
Double crochet (dc)
Double crochet 2 together (dc2tog)
Shell stitch
Single crochet (sc)
Single crochet 2 together (sc2tog)
Slip stitch (sl st)

Instructions

Ch 22.

Row 1: Dc in 4th ch and in each ch across row.

Row 2: Ch 1, turn. 1 sc in each of first 5 dc, ch 5, sk 3 dc, 1 sc in each of next 5 dc, ch 5, sk 3 dc, 1 sc in each of last 4 sc.

Row 3: Ch 3, turn. 1 dc in each of next 2 sc, sk 2 sc, make 7 dc in ch-5 lp, sk 2 sc, 2 dc in next sc, sk 2 sc, 7 dc in next ch-5 lp, sk 2 sc, 1 dc in each of next 2 sc, 1 dc in last sc of row.

Row 4: Ch 3, turn. 1 dc in next 2 dc, ch 3, sk first 3 dc of 7-dc shell, 1 sc in next dc of shell (4th dc of shell), ch 3, sk last 3 dc of shell, 1 dc in each of next 2 dc, ch 3, sk first 3 dc of next 7-dc shell, ch 3, 1 sc in 4th dc of shell, ch 3, sk last 3 dc of shell, 1 dc in each of last 3 sts of row.

Row 5: Ch 3, turn. 1 dc in each st across row.

Row 6: Ch 1, turn. 1 sc in each of first 5 dc, ch 5, sk 3 dc, 1 sc in each of next 5 dc, ch 5, sk 3 dc, 1 sc in each of last 6 sc.

Row 7: Ch 3, turn. 1 dc in each of next 2 sc, sk 3 sc, make 7 dc in ch-5 lp, sk 2 sc, 2 dc in next sc, sk 2 sc, 7 dc in next ch-5 lp, sk 2 sc, 1 dc in each of next 2 sc, 1 dc in last sc of row. Ch 3, turn.

Row 8: 1 dc in next 2 dc, ch 3, sk first 3 dc of 7-dc shell, 1 sc in next dc of shell (4th dc of shell), ch 3, sk last 3 dc of shell, 1 dc in each of next 2 dc, ch 3, sk first 3 dc of next 7-dc shell, ch 3, 1 sc in 4th dc of shell, ch 3, sk last 3 dc of shell, 1 dc in each of last 3 sts of row. Ch 3, turn.

Row 9: 1 dc in each st and ch across row.

Row 10: 1 sc in each of first 5 dc, ch 5, sk 3 dc, 1 sc in each of next 5 dc, ch 5, sk 3 dc, 1 sc in each of last 4 sc. Ch 3, turn.

Row 11: 1 dc in each of next 2 sc, sk 3 sc, make 7 dc in ch-5 lp, sk 2 sc, 2 dc in next sc, sk 2 sc, 7 dc in next ch-5 lp, sk 2 sc, 1 dc in each of next 2 sc, 1 dc in last sc of row. Ch 3, turn.

Row 12: 1 dc in next 2 dc, ch 3, sk first 3 dc of 7-dc shell, 1 sc in next dc of shell (4th dc of shell), ch 3, sk last 3 dc of shell, 1 dc in each of next 2 dc, ch 3, sk first 3 dc of next 7-dc shell, ch 3, 1 sc in 4th dc of shell, ch 3, sk last 3 dc of shell, 1 dc in each of last 3 sts of row. Ch 3, turn.

Row 13: 1 dc in each st and ch across row.

Row 14: 1 sc in each of first 5 dc, ch 5, sk 3 dc, 1 sc in each of next 5 dc, ch 5, sk 3 dc, 1 sc in each of last 4 sc. Ch 3, turn.

Row 15: 1 dc in each of next 2 dc, sk 2 sc, make 7 dc in ch-5 lp, sk 2 sc, 2 dc in next 2 sc, sk 2 sc, 7 dc in next ch-5 lp, sk 3 sc, 1 dc in each sc to end of row.

Row 16: 1 dc in next 2 dc, ch 3, sk first 3 dc of 7-dc shell, 1 sc in next dc of shell (4th dc of shell), ch 3, sk last 3 dc of shell, 1 dc in each of next 2 dc, ch 3, sk first 3 dc of next 7-dc shell, ch 3, 1 sc in 4th dc of shell, ch 3, sk last 3 dc of shell, 1 dc in each of last 3 sts of row.

Rows 17–28: Rep rows 2–5 until mini scarf measures approx 14 in. Ch 3, turn.

Row 29: 1 dc in each of next 2 dc, dc2tog over next 2 ch, 1 dc in next sc, 1 dc in each of next 3 ch, 1 dc in each of next 2 dc, dc2tog over next 2 ch, 1 dc in each st and ch until end of row.

Row 30: Sc2tog (reduce sc) as follows: Draw up a lp in each of next 2 dc, yo, draw up lp through all lps on hook. 1 sc in each of next 16 dc, sc2tog over next 2 sc. Ch 1, turn.

Row 31: Sc2tog over first 2 sc, 1 sc in each sc until last 2 sc, sc2tog over last 2 sc. Ch 1, turn.

Row 32: Sc2tog over first 2 sc, 1 sc in each of next 2 sc, sc2tog over next 2 sc, 1 sc in each of next 3 sc, sc2tog over next 2 sc, 1 sc in next sc, sc2tog over last 2 sc. Ch 1, turn.

Continued on next page.

Row 33: 1 sc in each of first 4 sc, sc2tog over next 2 sc, 1 sc in each sc to end of row. Ch 1, turn.

Row 34: 1 sc in each of first 3 sc, sc2tog over next 2 sc, 1 sc in next sc, sc2tog over next 2 sc, 1 sc in last sc. Ch 1, turn.

Row 35: 1 sc in each of first 2 sc, sc2tog over next 2 sc, 1 sc in each of last 2 sc. Ch 1, turn.

Row 36: 1 sc in each sc across row.

Rows 37–54: 1 sc in each sc across row. Fasten off, leaving a long tail to sew. Bend it inwards toward the wrong side, and, threading blunt needle with leftover tail, sew it to the row above the beginning row (row 36) to form a lp. Weave in tail.

Opposite side

Join yarn to the other end of the mini scarf.

Row 1: Rep row 30 of opposite side.

Row 2: Rep row 31 of opposite side.

Row 3: Rep row 32 of opposite side.

Row 4: Rep row 33 of opposite side.

Row 5: Rep row 34 of opposite side.

Row 6: Rep row 35 of opposite side.

Rows 7–8: 1 sc in each sc across row. Ch 1, turn.

Rows 9–10: 1 sc in each sc across row. Ch 1, turn.

Rows 11–12: 1 sc in each sc across row. Ch 1, turn.

Row 13 (increase row): Make 2 sc in first sc of row, 1 sc in next sc, 2 sc in each of next 2 sc, 1 sc in next sc, 2 sc in last sc. Ch 1, turn.

Row 14: 2 sc in first sc, 1 sc in each sc across until you reach last sc, 2 sc in last sc. Ch 1, turn.

Row 15: 1 sc in each of first 2 sc, 2 sc in next sc, 1 sc in each of next 2 sc, 2 sc in next sc, 1 sc in each of next 2 sc, 2 sc in next sc, 1 sc in next sc, 2 sc in last sc of row. Ch 1, turn.

Row 16: 1 sc in each sc across. Ch 4, turn (counts as first dc plus ch 1 of next row).

Row 17 (edging fan): Sk next sc, 1 dc in next sc, ch 1, sk next sc, 1 dc in next sc, ch 1, sk next 2 sc, 1 dc, ch 2, 1 dc in next sc, ch 1, sk next 2 sc, 1 dc in next sc, ch 1, sk next sc, 1 dc in next sc, ch 1, sk next sc, 1 dc in last sc. Ch 4, turn (counts as first dc plus ch 1 of next row).

Row 18: Sk to 2nd ch-sp, 1 dc in that ch-sp, 1 dc in next dc, 3 dc in next ch-sp, 1 dc in next dc, 3 dc in next ch-sp, 1 dc in next ch-sp, ch 1, 1 dc in last dc of row. Ch 4, turn (counts as first dc and ch 1 of next row).

Row 19: Sk next ch-sp, 1 dc in next dc, ch 3, sk next 4 dc, [1 dc in next dc, ch 2] 4 times, ch 3, sk next 3 dc, 1 dc in next dc, ch 1, 1 dc in last dc. Fasten off and weave in tail.

Opposite side (edging fan)

Join yarn to the end of the lp you made on opposite side of mini scarf.

Row 1: Working on the right side and inserting hook through both thicknesses of edge of loop formed, rep edging for opposite side of mini scarf. Fasten off. Weave in tail.